ANIMALS
That Make a Difference!

Cougars

J Smith

Explore other books at:
WWW.ENGAGEBOOKS.COM

VANCOUVER, B.C.

WWW.ENGAGEBOOKS.COM

Chimpanzees: Level 3
Animals That Make a Difference!
Smith, J,
Text © 2023 Engage Books
Design © 2023 Engage Books

Edited by: A.R. Roumanis,
Sarah Harvey, Melody Sun, and Ashley Lee
Design by: Mandy Christiansen

Text set in Arial Regular.
Chapter headings set in Nathaniel-19.

FIRST EDITION / FIRST PRINTING

LIBRARY AND ARCHIVES CANADA CATALOGUING IN PUBLICATION

Title: Cougars / Adelaide Wilder.
Names: Smith, J, author.
Description: Series statement: Animals that make a difference

Identifiers: Canadiana (print) 20230448526 | Canadiana (ebook) 20230448534
ISBN 978-1-77476-820-4 (hardcover)
ISBN 978-1-77476-821-1 (softcover)
ISBN 978-1-77476-822-8 (epub)
ISBN 978-1-77476-823-5 (pdf)
ISBN 978-1-77878-134-6 (audio)

Subjects:
LCSH: Puma—Juvenile literature.
LCSH: Human-animal relationships—Juvenile literature.

Classification: LCC QL737.C23 W56 2023 | DDC J599.75/24—DC23

This project has been made possible in part
by the Government of Canada.

Canada

Contents

What Are Cougars?

Cougars are part of the big cat family. They are related to cheetahs, lions, and tigers. Cougars are even related to house cats!

Cougars are large predators. That means they hunt and eat other animals. They are also **carnivores**. Other names for cougars are mountain lions, pumas, panthers, painters, and ghost cats.

KEY WORD

Carnivores: animals that only eat other animals.

Cougars need to eat about twenty pounds (9 kilograms) of meat every day.

A Closer Look

Cougars are usually tan, gray, silver, or brown. Adult cougars can grow up to 8 feet (2.4 meters) long, from their nose to the tip of their tail. They have white snouts and black tips on their ears and tails.

Cougars have great balance thanks to their long and heavy tails. By using their tail, cougars can easily stalk, pounce, run, and climb.

Cougars have strong back legs that help them jump long distances.

Cougars also have claws that pull back into their toes when not in use.

Where Do Cougars Live?

The only time cougars stay in one place is when they are raising their young. Female cougars build homes, called dens, to stay in with their babies. Cougars build dens in caves, under shrubs, and even under loose tree stumps.

Cougars are mostly found in South America and western North America. Some live in cold areas like the Yukon in northern Canada. Others can be found as far south as Argentina.

Yukon

North America

Pacific Ocean

Atlantic Ocean

South America

Argentina

0 2,000 miles

0 4,000 kilometers

N

Legend
- Land
- Ocean

Antarctica

9

What Do Cougars Eat?

Cougars eat all kinds of animals. This includes birds, lizards, fish, bugs, and other **mammals**. They like to attack by surprise from behind or above. This helps them take down large animals like elk and deer.

KEY WORD

Mammals: animals with warm blood and bones in their backs.

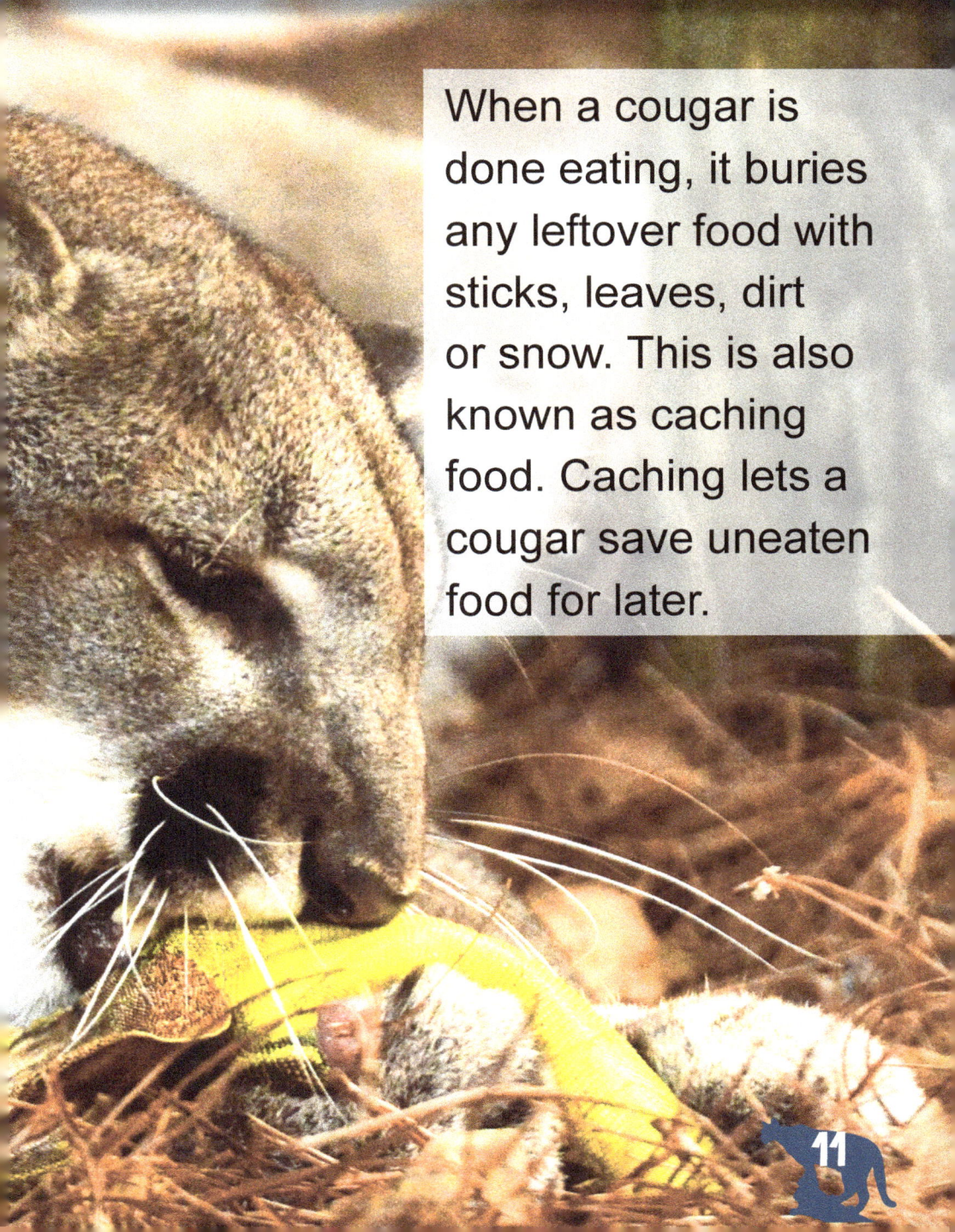

When a cougar is done eating, it buries any leftover food with sticks, leaves, dirt or snow. This is also known as caching food. Caching lets a cougar save uneaten food for later.

How Do Cougars Talk To Each Other?

Unlike lions and tigers, cougars do not roar at all. They purr! These big cats also growl, hiss, snarl, yip, and shriek to talk to each other.

Female cougars yowl to attract the attention of male cougars. This yowling is also sometimes called caterwauling. It can sound similar to a woman screaming or a baby crying.

Cougar Life Cycle

Baby cougars are called kittens or cubs. They stay close to their dens for the first two months after being born.

When they are between one and two years old, young cougars leave home in search of their own land.

Most cougars reach adulthood at around three years old.

Adult cougars do not like to share land. They prefer to find their own area where other cougars do not live.

Cougars can live 10 to 20 years in the wild, and even longer when in human care.

Curious Facts About Cougars

Cougars can jump as far as 40 feet (13 meters). That is as long as a city bus!

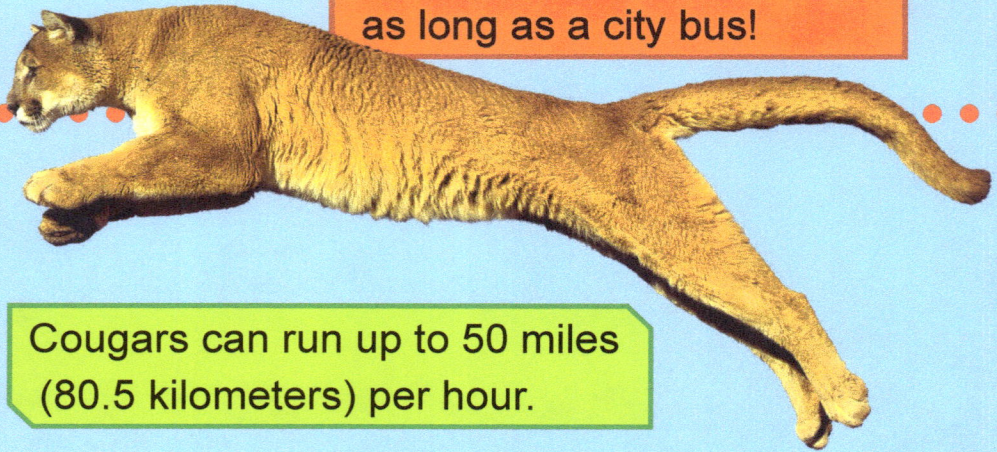

Cougars can run up to 50 miles (80.5 kilometers) per hour.

Cougar cubs are born with spotted coats. Their spots help them blend in with the shadows made by leaves and shrubs.

Cougars are great swimmers, but like many cats, they do not like to get wet!

Each adult cougar needs around 100 square miles (258 square km) of land to live well.

Cougars have poor senses of smell. They rely on their eyes and ears for hunting.

17

Kinds of Cougars

There are North American cougars and South American cougars. North American cougars live across Canada and central and southern North America. Their common **habitats** are wooded areas, wetland areas, and forests. They have darker coats and mostly hunt elk and deer.

KEY WORD

Habitats: natural places where plants and animals live.

South American cougars are found in countries such as Colombia, Venezuela, Argentina, and Chile. They have lighter coats than North American Cougars, and they hunt all kinds of animals. They have been known to eat reptiles, rodents, sloths, and even bear cubs.

How Cougars Help Earth

Herbivores are animals that eat only plants. Cougars hunt a lot of herbivores. By hunting them, cougars keep the number of herbivores under control. If there are too many herbivores, they may eat a lot of plants and trees. By hunting herbivores, cougars help keep the **ecosystem** healthy.

KEY WORD

Ecosystem: a community of living and nonliving things that work together.

Cougars also eat leftovers from other animals. By eating dead animals, cougars help recycle **nutrients** and stop diseases from spreading. This keeps the environment healthy.

KEY WORD

Nutrients: things in food that help people, animals, and plants live and grow.

How Cougars Help Other Animals

Some animals need plenty of plants and trees for food. Some animals also make their homes out of different parts of plants. When there are not enough plants, animals can go hungry. Some will have a hard time finding a place to live.

By hunting herbivores, cougars help protect the growth of a lot of plants and trees. Other animals that need plants and trees to live will have enough of them to eat and make homes out of.

How Cougars Help Humans

Trees create over a quarter of Earth's oxygen. Humans depend on trees and other plants for the air they breathe. So when cougars protect trees from herbivores, it helps humans too!

Having cougars in an ecosystem often means that the environment is healthy and safe. People keep an eye on how many cougars there are and where they go. This helps them learn about how well the environment is doing.

Cougars in Danger

Most kinds of cougas are safe and healthy for now, but some groups are endangered. This means that there are not many of them left. The Florida Panther and the Costa Rican Puma are endangered now.

There are only around 160 Florida Panthers left in the wild.

Cougars need lots of space to travel, hunt, and sleep. But things like highway construction and tree cutting are forcing cougars out of their habitat. This might cause the number of cougars to become smaller in the future.

How to Help Cougars

Cougars are often in danger when they run into humans. They may be killed by animal control officers if they wander too close to cities and towns. It is still legal to hunt cougars in many places. Avoiding cougars is the best way to keep them safe.

Always go with an adult if you go into the wilderness. Be extra careful at sunrise and sunset. That is when cougars are most active. Attach a bell to your clothes or your backpack.

Cougars will usually try to avoid humans if they know where they are. If you have a pet with you, keep it nearby at all times.

Quiz

Test your knowledge of cougars by answering the following questions. The questions are based on what you have read in this book. The answers are listed on the bottom of the next page.

1 Are cougars carnivores or herbivores?

2 Where can cougars be found?

3 What is also known as caching food?

4 What are baby cougars called?

5 How fast can cougars run?

6 What kinds of cougars are endangered now?

Explore other books in the Animals That Make a Difference series

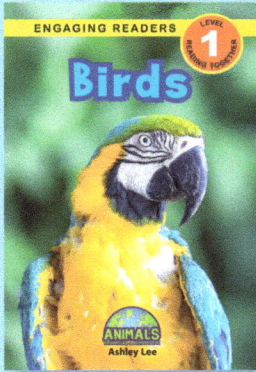

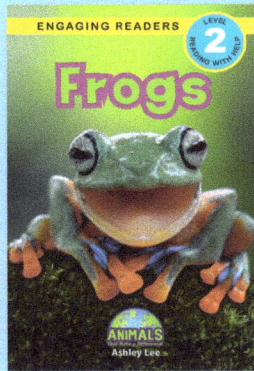
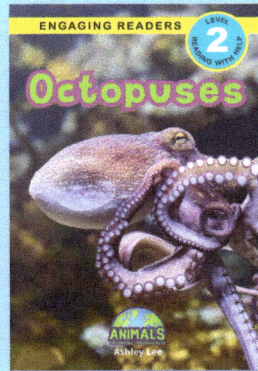

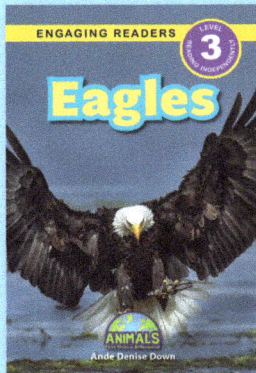
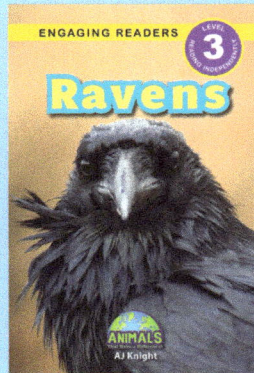
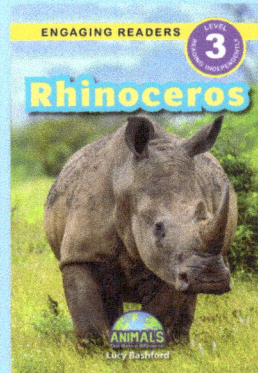

Visit www.engagebooks.com to explore more Engaging Readers.